No part of this book may be reproduced, distributed, or transmitted in any form or by any means, including photocopying, recording, or other electronic or mechanical methods, without the prior written permission of the author, except in the case of brief quotations embodied in critical reviews and certain other noncommercial uses permitted by copyright law.

ISBN: 978-1-0689087-1-2
First Edition: January 2025

Copyright © 2025 by Shannon Mckay
All rights reserved.

For all of the missing

muddle boots of the world

Play Hide N Seek with me!

I'm hiding on every page.

Mud on his boots,

mud in her hair.

Mud on the cows,

And on his hat.

Mud on the chickens,

and on the cat.

My sister got covered.

She started to shout.

We couldn't dig her up.

So she swam her way out!

My Father is furious.

He can't get us to leave.

With our pet pig Steve.

www.ingramcontent.com/pod-product-compliance
Lightning Source LLC
Chambersburg PA
CBHW042130040426
42450CB00003B/144